PARTS OF A PLANT

A Look at Seeds and Beans

Lindsey Lowe

KidHaven PUBLISHING

Published in 2020 by
KidHaven Publishing, an Imprint of
Greenhaven Publishing, LLC
353 3rd Avenue
Suite 255
New York, NY 10010

For Brown Bear Books Ltd:
Text and Editor: Lindsey Lowe
Children's Publisher: Anne O'Daly
Design Manager: Keith Davis
Picture Manager: Sophie Mortimer

Picture Credits
t=top, c=center, b=bottom, l=left, r=right
Interior: iStock: 5t, avtg 16, joangran 17t, jeanro 12b, mauibo 12-13, Gemma Redding 15t; Public Domain: Shams bahari 11b; Shutterstock: 4r, 5b, 7cl, 7bl, 13b, 17b, 18-19, 19br, 19bc, 20, 21, Nikola Bilic 18br, BlueOrange Studio 10, Diegomez 14, Jason Finn, 9t, Bess Hamitii 8, D Kucharski 7bc, LiliGraphie 6-7, lovleyday 11t, Somyot Mali-Hagm 15b, Kanoksak Meamsum 7br, Ruud Morijn 9b, Maks Narodenko 4l, Ermak Okana 19bl, Sajeed Pecharut 19bll, Yuri Samsonov 6br, Spainic 18bl, Anton Starikov 19brr, YamabikaY 6bl.
All other photos and artwork, Brown Bear Books.

Cataloging-in-Publication Data

Names: Lowe, Lindsey.
Title: A look at seeds and beans / Lindsey Lowe.
Description: New York : KidHaven Publishing, 2020. | Series: Parts of a plant | Includes glossary and index.
Identifiers: ISBN 9781534533776 (pbk.) | ISBN 9781534533790 (library bound) | ISBN 9781534533783 (6 pack) | ISBN 9781534533806 (ebook)
Subjects: LCSH: Seeds--Juvenile literature. | Beans--Juvenile literature. | Plant anatomy--Juvenile literature.
Classification: LCC QK661.L694 2020 | DDC 581.4'67--dc23

Manufactured in the United States of America

CPSIA Compliance Information: Batch #BW20KL
For further information contact Greenhaven Publishing LLC, New York, New York at 1-844-317-7404.

Contents

What Are Seeds?

Seeds are plant starter kits. Each seed contains a tiny root and stem. They grow to make a new plant.

The seed also contains a store of food. The young plant uses this to grow. The seed has a tough outer coat to protect the baby plant. When the plant is big enough, the seed coat splits open. The root and stem appear.

Seed Protectors

Seeds grow inside a fruit. The fruit keeps the seed safe. Some fruits, like avocado, have one seed inside. Others, like watermelon, have lots of seeds. Pea pods are fruits. Walnuts are hard, dry fruits.

THAT'S AMAZING!

The coco de mer palm tree has a giant fruit. Inside the hard, dry fruit (see right) there's an enormous seed. The seed can grow more than 12 inches (30 cm) long. It can weigh up to 50 pounds (20 kilograms). That's the weight of three bowling balls!

Beans

Beans are seeds. They belong to a family of plants called legumes. These are plants that grow pods with seeds inside them. Legumes include lentils, chickpeas, soybeans, peas, and peanuts.

Kinds of Seeds

Seeds come in all shapes, sizes, and colors. There are about a million different types of seeds.

A palm tree makes a few very big seeds. They are called coconuts. Orchid flowers make millions of tiny seeds that look like dust. A carrot seed has tiny spines. The seed of a hazelnut is inside a hard shell. The seed of a plum is inside the pit inside the fruit.

Different Seeds

Here are some different kinds of seeds. Some can be eaten. Foxglove and plum seeds are poisonous. You should never eat them.

Carrot Seed

Hazelnut

THAT'S AMAZING!

Not every seed made by a plant grows into another plant. An oak tree can have 10,000 acorns in a year. Each acorn contains a single seed. But only about 100 seeds grow into new trees. Oak trees can live to be 1,000 years old. In that time they can produce as many as 10 million acorns!

Most oak trees are 50 years old before they produce a big crop of acorns.

Peas

Foxglove Seeds

Plum

Spreading Seeds

Seeds grow best if they sprout away from the parent plant. They travel in different ways.

Some seeds are blown by the wind. Other seeds are carried by water. Some plants, like peas, have seed pods. The pod swells and bursts. The seeds fly away through the air. Animals and birds also help to spread seeds. They eat the fruits and the seeds come out in their poop.

A dandelion seed has a mini parachute. When the wind blows, the seeds are blown away from the plant. They land and grow.

THAT'S AMAZING!

The tumbleweed is an unusual plant. When it spreads its seeds, it is not just the seeds that move! Each plant makes between 20,000 and 50,000 papery seeds. When the wind blows, the stem of the plant breaks away from the roots. The wind rolls the plant along the ground. As it tumbles, the plant spreads its seeds!

Hitching a Ride

Some seeds are carried by animals. The fruits that hold burdock seeds have tiny hooks and spikes. They catch on the fur of passing animals. Other seeds have sticky coats that stick to an animal's fur.

How Seeds Grow

Seeds need water and sunlight to grow. A new plant grows quickly after the seed has sprouted.

The seed soaks up water and swells. The seed coat splits open and a tiny root appears. The root grows and takes water from the ground. The first shoots appear above the ground.

Coconuts

The coconut palm spreads its seeds using the ocean. This washed-up coconut has started to sprout. The seed contains enough food for the young plant to grow.

The Right Time

The weather must be just right for a seed to sprout. Seeds need warmth and sunlight. If the weather is too cold or too dry, a new plant will die. Most seeds start to sprout and grow in warm spring sunshine.

THAT'S AMAZING!

Sometimes seeds wait in the ground for years before they start to grow. In 2012, a team of Russian scientists successfully grew a plant from a 32,000-year-old seed. It had been buried in Siberia by an Ice Age squirrel!

Seeds and Birds

Seeds are tough. Birds that eat seeds need strong beaks to crack the seeds open.

Birds eat fresh seeds. They also store some for later. They collect seeds and bury them in the summer. They dig them up again when they need food in the winter.

Bird Cupboard

The acorn woodpecker stores acorns for the winter. It drills tiny holes in tree trunks with its beak. It puts an acorn in each hole. The bird has food when acorns are hard to find.

Burying Seeds

Some birds can bury up to 1,000 seeds a day! Sometimes the bird forgets about them. This is good for the seeds. They stay in the ground and grow into new plants.

THAT'S AMAZING!

Birds called finches eat a lot of seeds. Seeds make up about half of their diet. Different types of finches have different-shaped beaks. Greenfinches like this one have short, thick beaks for eating tough sunflower seeds. The tips of a crossbill's beak cross over. This helps it to pull seeds out of pine cones. A hawkfinch's beak is so strong it can crack open a cherry pit!

Seeds and Rodents

Some small animals eat hard seeds. They break open the shell with their long front teeth.

Mice, rats, beavers, and squirrels are all rodents. They have very strong front teeth. They can chew through the hard shells of nuts like walnuts and hazelnuts. They make a hole and eat the seed inside.

Agouti

The agouti is a rodent about the size of a rabbit. It lives in forests in South America. Its sharp, tough teeth can crack open hard Brazil nuts to eat.

Fall Harvest

In fall, hazelnuts drop from hazel trees. Wood mice take the nuts back to their nests to eat in winter. Some of the nuts are left uneaten. In the spring, the seeds start to grow into new hazel trees.

THAT'S AMAZING!

The seeds of castor oil plants are coated with a special oil that attracts ants. The ants drag the seeds to their underground nests. They feed on the oil but leave the seeds. The seeds have been planted underground by the ants and are ready to grow!

Cereal Seeds

Seeds are grown for people to eat. Cereal plants are the main food crops around the world.

Wheat, corn, oats, rye, barley, millet, and rice are all kinds of grasses. They are called cereals. The seeds of cereals are called grains. The grains grow in clumps, or ears, at the tops of the stems. Farmers plant cereals every year. When the seeds are ripe, they are harvested.

The Harvest

Wheat seeds turn golden when they are ripe. Huge machines cut off the stems and collect the grain. It is turned into flour and used to make bread, pasta, and cakes.

THAT'S AMAZING!

Rice is the main food crop for more than half the people in the world. In China, the word for rice is the same as the word for food! Most rice is grown in fields called paddies. The fields are flooded with water to help the rice grow.

Corn on the Cob

Corn grows on corncobs. The sweet corn seeds can be canned or cooked and eaten straight from the cob. Corn is also turned into flakes for breakfast cereals or ground to make flour.

Using Seeds

Nearly all cooking oils and spices come from seeds. Seeds are also turned into things people use.

Most seeds contain oil. People use plant oils for cooking, frying, and baking. The oils can be flavored with herbs and spices. Popular oils for cooking include sunflower oil, corn oil, grapeseed oil, and coconut oil.

Seeds for Flavor

Spices help to make food taste better. Here are some popular seeds that can be added to food. You can buy them in supermarkets. How many have you tried?

Caraway

Pepper

THAT'S AMAZING!

Some plant oils are used to make paint, glue, and cloth. Other plant oils are used to protect wood from moisture and heat. Scientists have discovered that fuel made from sunflower oil could be used to power cars in place of gasoline or diesel! The fuel is called biodiesel. It is a clean fuel. It may help to reduce air pollution from cars.

You need about 140 sunflowers to produce 35 pounds (15 kg) of seeds. This makes about 3 gallons (11 L) of oil.

Grow It!

Cress seeds are easy to grow. Sow the seeds in small plastic pots or trays, or use an empty eggshell. Draw a face on the shell and watch its cress "hair" grow!

Here's How

- Buy a packet of cress seeds from a garden store, supermarket, or online.
- Find a clean food packaging tray or yogurt container. Put some damp cotton batting or paper towel in the bottom.
- Sprinkle the seeds over the damp cotton or paper towel. You don't need to space them out too much. They can grow close together in clumps.
- Check every few hours. Keep the cotton or paper towel damp by spraying lightly with water.
- Small white roots will start to grow after just a few hours. After about 5 days, the seedlings will be around 1.5 inches (3.8 cm) tall and ready to pick.
- Snip the stems off when you are ready to eat them. They will not keep once they have been cut.

Cook It!

Sunflower seeds add a nutty crunch to these oat cookies!

- 1 cup butter, softened
- 1 cup white sugar
- 1 cup light brown sugar
- 2 eggs, beaten
- 1 tsp vanilla extract
- 2 cups flour
- 1 tsp baking soda
- ½ tsp baking powder
- ¼ tsp salt
- 2 cups rolled oats
- 1 cup flaked coconut
- 1 cup unsalted, roasted sunflower seeds

Here's How

1. Preheat the oven to 350°F (175°C). Beat the butter and sugars together in a bowl until light and fluffy. Add the eggs and vanilla and beat again.
2. In another bowl, mix the flour, baking soda, baking powder, and salt. Stir this dry mixture into the butter mixture.
3. Stir in the oats, coconut flakes, and most of the sunflower seeds.
4. Put tablespoonfuls of the mixture onto an ungreased cookie sheet.
5. Bake for 8 to 10 minutes. When they have cooled a bit, press sunflower seeds into the top of each cookie. Leave the cookies to cool on a wire rack.

WARNING

Most cooking involves chopping ingredients and heating them in some way. Be careful as you cook and make sure an adult kitchen assistant is around to help!

Glossary

acorn The nut of an oak tree.

cereal A grass plant with seeds that can be eaten.

fruit The part of a plant that contains its seed.

grain A seed that can be eaten, like the seed of cereal plants.

harvest To pick what has been planted and grown in the ground.

nut A fruit with a hard shell.

pod The oval-shaped part of a plant that contains seeds.

rodent A small, furry animal with two long front teeth.

seed coat The tough outer layer of a seed.

shoot The stem and leaves of a plant.

Further Resources

Books

Aloian, Molly. *What Are Seeds?* New York: Crabtree Publishing, 2012.

DK, Smithsonian. *Trees, Leaves, Flowers, and Seeds* (Smithsonian). New York: DK Children, 2019.

Dickmann, Nancy. *Q & A About Plants* (Curious Nature). New York: Powerkids Press, 2017.

Stewart, Melissa. *A Seed Is the Start.* Washington, D.C.: National Geographic Children's Books, 2018.

Websites

https://kids.kiddle.co/Seed

https://easyscienceforkids.com/all-about-germination/

Publisher's note to educators and parents: Our editors have carefully reviewed these websites to ensure that they are suitable for students. Many websites change frequently, however, and we cannot guarantee that a site's future contents will continue to meet our high standards of quality and educational value. Be advised that students should be closely supervised whenever they access the Internet.

Index